Hidden Thoughts

THE THOUGHTS BEHIND THE SECRETS

UNIQUE WRITEZ

PRINTED IN THE UNTIED STATES OF AMERICA

ISBN: 978-1-64606-696-4

Contents

Visit Unique Writez's Facebook for the latest news and updates.

Facebook Group: https://bit.ly/2JK8XMy
Instagram: _theperfectflaw
Twitter: ThePerfect_Flaw
Facebook: https://bit.ly/2JElroV

Acknowledgments

Lord, I'm going to try and keep this short.

First, let me give all praise to God for my ability to complete this book.

I would also like to thank Nikki Flowers, my publisher. You saw something in me, something in my writings, that even I didn't see when I first began this journey. You pushed me when I was ready to completely give up. You were on it. I am forever grateful for this opportunity to work with you. I love you beyond words and I appreciate you!

To my children, Levar, Kaiden, and Kaidence, Mommy does this all for you!

To both of my mothers and my granny—thank you for getting me writing supplies, books, and everything else to help me begin my love for writing. I love y'all to life.

To siblings Sheem, Quai, Callie, Baby Rav, and Lanelle—thank you for all of the nights y'all read my poems and snippets in the wee hours of the morning. I can't thank y'all enough for encouraging me.

Raven and Shod, my cousins, y'all read every line, saw every tear, and felt every emotion, baby!

To my friends, Lish, Mia, Nai, and Moo, y'all kept the pen in my hand!

Aunt Mel, your advice and support picked me up on days I felt I just couldn't do it any longer. Thank you for keeping me going.

Greez, baby, you are my biggest motivator. I would have never started this book without you, love. Throughout this journey, you have kept me grounded and kept me sane, giving all the love, encouragement, and support since day one. You're up next, my love!

Daniel, you've watched this come to life, even after 10+ years of writing. You'll never know how much you mean to me!

Mer, since I was twelve, you ain't never left my side. Most of the events that inspired my writing, you've seen me go through firsthand. Along the way, you always reminded me that I could do anything I put my mind to. Well, here we are—it's complete!

A huge thank you goes to Marla Duncan. Our video chats mean the world to me. You were always there to help me tweak poems, while telling me leave others be because they were perfect. You supported me 100 percent without knowing me. Y'all, this girl bought books, pens, came to my open mics, and shared my writings when no one else would!

Da, I can still remember what you told me when I came to you. You told me, 'Do it! You're good enough. You always have been.' Those words have stayed at the forefront of my mind forever. I love you.

To everyone else that has supported me and continues to support and encourage me, I truly thank you from the bottom of my heart. I hope you enjoy finding out the thoughts behind my secrets.

If I forgot anyone, I apologize. Please blame my mind and not my heart. I love you all so much.

The Creation

In the beginning God created the Heavens and the
Earth
Then there was me, and the life God chose for my
siblings and I.
This is it!
How did it come to this?
The flame in the girl you knew is no longer lit
Nothing but darkness surrounds her in this empty
pit!
No one saw the signs
So it seemed very sudden when the decision was
made.

Everyone assumed she was happy
Truth is, she's been self-destructing from the loss of
her innocence.
She talked to God
But I don't think he heard her.
She stepped out on a leap of faith
And her life turned to ruin.
Anything and everything could be a trigger
Lost in her own mind as the hidden thoughts keep
her in a surprise
One foot in Hell
She's ready to give up,
The blood stains the tub,
The alcohol and pills settle within
While the sun sets on her
Once Upon a Time.

When the Door Closes

I can hear the loud knocks of my best friend kicking and screaming at the door in a panic. I know by now she got my text and is worried to death. I took her key to my apartment days ago, so I know she can't get in.

This is it for me, I remind myself. Tired, I gave up completely.

I sent out all my goodbyes to the people who meant the most to me before I swallowed a handful of opiates, followed by a pint of Henny—straight. If I was going to go out, I was going to go out in style, and I was damn sure going to drink the finest while doing it.

The taste sent a slight chill down my body, leaving an awful aftertaste. Lighting my cigarette, I lay my head back on the tub and try to relax myself. I was ready for it to be over. I silently hoped the process would be quick, smooth, and painless.

This will be my last worry. At last, all others will be laid to rest with me, I thought to myself as I waited for the darkness to take me. No more stress, heartache, or fighting with my inner self, which has never healed from past hurt. No more being haunted by the demons in my sleep, or the shadows when I'm awake… My thoughts consumed me as I slid in and out of consciousness.

In truth, I tried to keep them at bay all these years, but sadly, it just didn't work. Now it will all just fade to black, drifting into oblivion, no longer a worry on my mind.

Little Girl Lost

She screams

She cries

Begging and pleading in-between whines

"Let me out, I want to be free."

She constantly yells at me!

I, in my adult form, am too afraid to go back

Too afraid the demons she suppresses will come

back to haunt her,

Locking her away was better than the reality I'd

have to face physically.

I'm a grown ass woman

But locked inside is where that little broken girl lies

I know in order for her to heal
I'd have to open the seal
It'll get ugly before there is beauty
Though, I don't know if I'm ready to do that to me
Am I ready to lie in my own mess of ugly
Repaint the picture that is my life
Am I ready to mourn the loss of the little broken
girl who was lost?
Am I ready to allow the inner me to peek at what I
grew up to be?
I just don't know if I'm ready to do that to me just
yet.

Behind Closed Doors

My body was warm and tingly as the intoxication took over, a sense of peace flowing through me.

A vision of my grandmother was there in the light, waiting with open arms for me. I tried running to her, but she was too far. In the distance, I could hear her call out to me. *"Turn back! It's not your time yet, baby. It's not your time."*

I tried to scream my reply. *"I can't do this any longer. I don't want to."* Crying out, I begged for death to just soothe me.

Suddenly, I was back, unable to move my numb body. Hearing the locks turn, I knew my best friend was in my apartment. I could hear her frantically screaming and yelling at my cousin. "Ree get a fucking rag, she's bleeding out!"

Slitting my wrists, I awaited the release. It was such a rush when I hit the vein. Everything was flooding out as the blood dripped down my hands. As if in a dream, I could hear my cousins screaming, pacing back and forth, their cries echoing off the walls. "I can't do this shit! Why would Michelle do this to herself?"

Out of worry and frustration, Booker tells everyone, "Move the fuck back, y'all aren't no fucking help! She could die while y'all screaming!"

Meanwhile, I'm just sitting here, slipping in and out, silently begging for them to just let me die.

Love Drunk

I didn't wanna do this

No, not like this

The more I ran from it

The more your love had me gripped with a closed

fist

Pulling me closer

See, your love gets me drunk

And I'm sick when I'm sober

A hangover when it's over

No matter how hard I tried to stay away

I still wound up sipping the bottle

When will I learn this is something I can't continue
to partake in
Every time, I wake up without you, my heart is
aching
For the love of a broken man
Who just doesn't understand
All I'm trying to do is love you
All of you
Even the parts of you with issues and baggage
I'm willing to help you unload it
As much as I try, I can't process any reason why
You say I shouldn't have you!
But you love me, right ?
Tell me, is it me you think of when the sun rises
Or the moon lights the night sky?
You wanna tell me how I should feel
You say maybe I should walk away
The truth still remains
I LOVE YOU ENOUGH TO STAY!

When the Door Opens

I should have waited a little longer to send that goodbye texts. I truly didn't want to live and I didn't want help. I tried to speak, I tried to tell them to leave me alone, but everything went black.

The next thing I knew, I woke up to bright lights, beeping machines, and my family and friends surrounding me with worried looks and tear-stained faces. I had no idea how long I'd been in this state, but there I was.

Tubes and IVs covered my body and my head was pounding. Glancing down, I found my wrists and feet were bound down to a bed. I was totally confused. *Why am I cuffed to the bed?*

"You've been out for two weeks because of the pills you took and the liquor you drank. It was a deadly combination. Between that and the loss of blood from cutting your wrists, it put you in a coma," Booker explained, with a sad tremble in his voice. Taking a deep breath, he continued. "I don't understand why you would do this, Michelle. What happened? What's going on with you? What were you thinking?" I could see the tears in his eyes, threatening to fall.

In a way, I guess everyone wants to understand that infamous question? Truth be told, there is no short answer as to how I got to this moment in time. My whole life had brought me to this point. Nobody had heard my cries, nobody cared about my story, but maybe, just maybe, it was time to tell my story! The good, the bad, and the ugly in between—all of it led to this point in my life.

Hidden Thoughts
THE THOUGHTS BEHIND MY SECRETS
TAKE ONE

Honestly, I was born with the odds stacked against me. I had no father and a drug addicted mother who loved me, but loved the drugs more. There are times I remember us being 'normal'. Of course, that was all before crack contaminated our lives. Despite everything, I thank God my mother had enough sense to give me to my Auntie, so she could raise me, as opposed to selling me into slavery for another hit.

In truth, a lot of my friends I had growing up in that era had day terrors, dreading the thought of going home. I was one of them, until my Auntie took me in.

Thinking back, my childhood was decent. At least I was able to live with family. I was a good kid, honor roll student; I had everything I wanted or needed. Though, that didn't stop the no home training having bullies outside where I lived, or at school that harassed me daily. Even with all that, I was good. I was the target of every joke. Fatty McFat Fat Michelle, Nappy Nap Nap, Whale Michelle—the list goes on and on. For years, I was tortured and humiliated.

I can still remember it like it was yesterday. In 4th grade my chest had started blooming and a group of popular boys surrounded me and took turns calling me names. It wasn't cool to have breasts back then, I guess. They would scream while lifting up my shirt, *'Fatty needs a bra now! Look!'*. Eventually, I was able to break through the group and run to the bathroom. Thinking back on it, I spent a lot of time in the bathroom stalls. I would run in there and just sit and cry until I heard the busses get called that would carry me home. I'd never felt so low, so angry and upset, in my entire life. That day I vowed to show them all that I wouldn't take any more crap from anyone!

Sadly, I believe that's when the start of myself-destructive behavior began. From that day on, I raged a war against myself and everyone else in my path. The only question that remained...

Would I survive my own destructive tendencies?

Enough!

Options are few, down on my knees
I plead to you spirits—my heart is way too heavy
It's too much for me alone to carry
I know I can't do this on my own
The battle is not mine
I've been told I need you now
Arms open wide
Fill me up, Lord
Make me whole
The burdens I carry are eating me alive
Lord, I need to release
I lay it all down at your feet

Hidden Secrets

I know I've come far, but I'm still far too weak
That's when a voice started to speak—
'My child, I set you free
Cast your sorrows upon me and leave
You will accept many things
Though, I will not allow you to accept DEFEAT
I know you are tired
So, it is me that will carry you through these dark
times
I have never left, nor forsaken thee
I need you to put all faith and glory in me
Just wait, and you will see
You are exactly where I want you to be
Now stand tall, you've got work to do.'

Hidden Thoughts
THE THOUGHTS BEHIND MY SECRETS
TAKE TWO

I held all my emotions in, becoming an evil genie, granting wishes from bottled up emotions. I became the person with a tough 'I don't care' shell, built as tough as they come. Over time, I learned how to protect myself from any hurt that could be heading my way. The following school year, I was suspended so much for fighting and arguing that I was hardly ever in school to get bullied. My grades began to slip and I didn't care.

Shit, they stopped bullying my ass and I even earned a little bit of respect on the playground. Everyone finally left me alone. My auntie, the teachers at school, and the principle wanted their sweet, little, innocent girl back, but it was too late. The mental damage had already been done and the new me was there to stay.

When I say my auntie tried everything she could to get through to me, I mean it. She went so far as to locking me up, beating the hell outta me, and locking me in my room all day. She had tried it all. Sadly, nothing got through to me. I wouldn't allow it.

It's odd—the universe has a funny way of showing you how tough you are and just how much your soul can bear. It wasn't until I was alone at night that I released all of my pent-up frustration and hurt.

Then, at the age of twelve, my body began to fill out. There I was, standing 4'6", 130 pounds, banging hips, a voluptuous booty and nearly a Ccup bra. Suddenly, the negative attention became a fierce torch. After that, I found myself hanging out with girls much older than me—fourteen, fifteen, sixteen years old. I never wanted to hang with my age group after getting a taste of being a young adult. Instead, I wanted desperately to be grown. I wanted a new life.

As I got older, I discovered peer pressure was a motherfucker. Thanks to my friends, drinking and smoking became my new coping mechanism, which only aided me further in my internal destruction. Before long, I was faithfully sneaking out to go drinking, I call myself having a boyfriend and was lying about my virginity.

Jay was the very first guy I ever loved. Boy, you couldn't tell me anything when it came to him. Jay was fifteen-years-old, six feet tall, and cut like a bag of dope. He had the cutest smile with the dreamiest eyes, and I couldn't believe it, that he wanted me. When he chose me, the girl everyone used to pick on, the girl with the low self-esteem, a lot of them hating ass ho's that bullied me were suddenly envying me from afar. Around Jay, everything disappeared. All of the ugliness in my life, the low self-esteem issues, the fact that my mother was an addict—it all ceased to exist.

Love Takes All

I'm sorry I brushed you off

I didn't realize I had to let my guard down to allow

new happiness

Stop assuming nothing would become of it

The feeling was so strong

I didn't know what to make of it

So naturally, I declined it

I was putting forth no effort

Unwilling to meet you halfway

You were pouring out your love

And I was running the other way

Declining phone calls

Hidden Secrets

Not in the mood to see you today

The more I pulled back

The harder you tried to reel me in

Your love swooping me up like the wind

I pray it's not too late

Let's not let this be the end

I put my guard down this time

LOVE WINS

Our chemistry is great

The vibes are amazing

I'll admit it's got me falling all in love

I can't even fake it

Ain't even been that long

And, baby, you got me wide open

Feeling crazy.

I hope the feeling is mutual

All you gotta do is say the word

And I'm all yours

For you, I'm willing to risk it all

I promise

I wanna be the one who loves you unconditionally♥

Random Thoughts

I sit here with this blank sheet
Waiting for my thoughts to manifest
What will I write this time around
I guess whatever scattered thoughts I can bring to
mind now
Although my thoughts are unclear
Sketchy, like a pencil on a blank canvas
Something down in me is speaking
It keeps repeating
"Pen to the pad is what you know, stop thinking and
let it flow!"
I hate when my mind is scattered this way

Hidden Secrets

I can't figure out what I'll say

Then it hits me

This one has to be spoken!

This is about a girl who looks put together

But beneath that mask she's just broken

Just like any other woman

She just wants to be seen

Every scar

Every broken piece

She still wants to be deemed

Beautiful!

To not be frowned upon for her short-comings

Instead, she wants to be uplifted

Even though she was broken and damaged

She's still a diamond

If you can look past the cracks

You'll see something magnificent

Nothing short of amazing

With the odds stacked against her

She's overcome each one!

The broken pieces are just a display of her strength

She's been through Hell and back to get to this
point!
Lonely days
Sleepless nights
Putting up a front day-to-day so people couldn't see
it.
She's finally gotten to a place of serenity
Most of her open wounds healed
Her smile is finally real
She laughs harder and loves deeper
She's finally at peace!
She is Me and I am She
Look past the display
And see my TRUE BEAUTY.

Hidden Thoughts
THE THOUGHTS BEHIND MY SECRETS
TAKE THREE

I had to be sneaky, Jay lived right down the street and if my auntie found out, all hell would break loose. She already hated his mama. She knew her from around the neighborhood bars, so there was no way in hell she'd let us be a couple. The Lord would have to strike her down before she would even entertain the thought. Knowing how my mama felt, we were left with no choice but to sneak in and out of closet doors. Which was okay by me.

For some reason, I just couldn't get enough of the way he smelled, the way he touched me, and the way he looked with that small dimple in his left cheek. I had to have him any chance I was able to get my hot ass away from my aunt. Some nights, I craved his flesh so badly I didn't care about the repercussions of my aunt. I guess deep down, I wanted to get caught. I wanted to put our sneaking around to an end.

The more confident I became sneaking out of the windows, the more elaborate my ambitious ways became. The boldness set in and before long, my friends and I were in my room drinking, smoking, and doing a lot of grinding into the wee hours of the morning. Thankfully, it was very rare that my aunt come into my room, but with the incense burning, I was able to hide the cigarette smoke. As soon as I knew my aunt was fast asleep with the drunken snore, my window was open for my friends to come in.

Jay and his friend would often slither through the bedroom window to hang out and then they would creep out the front door just before dawn. Lying in my room, we'd try to be silent while giving one another sucker bites on our necks. *Damn!* Jay was always looking good, and oh my goodness, he smelled even better. Just the aroma of his cologne drove me crazy, making my middle spot tingle. I would get so wrapped up in him that I wouldn't even realize how quickly the time would fly.

The hardest part of the morning was having to watch him walk away. Even though I knew it was only until night fell once again. Besides, I had to let him go before my aunt woke up. Not to mention, I needed to get ready for school.

One morning in particular, I ignored my first instinct and we laid back down for little bit longer. I wasn't willing to let the moment just yet. I wanted that moment to last forever. Two more seconds, that's all I wanted. Sadly, it was two seconds too long.

Right on cue, my auntie busted through my door to wake me up for school, just as the sun hit the middle of the sky. At first, she didn't see anyone because I hid Jay under the covers. My home girl relaxed because she was a regular over my house every day. I breathed a sigh of relief as my auntie started to walk out the door. I thought I had it made. I tried to hurry out the room behind her, but it was already too late. *WAP! WAP*! I got a backhand right upside my damn head. I had hidden Jay, but forgot to hide his shoes.

How could I have been that damn stupid?

"You got niggas up in my house, bitch!" she yelled at the top of her lungs. Two more blows to the face, quickly followed by blows to my body.

My friend was scared shitless. Not bothering to gather their belongings, the boys quickly jumped out the window. Just when I thought things couldn't get any worse, my friend's mom came to see what all the commotion was about. Seeing the beating I was taking my home girl quickly gathered her shit and took off out the room, running right into her biggest fan. *Her mother.* Confused at first, my friend's mother quickly realized what was going on as she listened to my aunt scream, "I'm going to kill you for disrespecting my house, bitch!"

It wouldn't be long before she felt my pain. The same ass kicking I was receiving from my auntie, her mother was now giving her. Her mother wailed on her just like my aunt was whooping my ass. The hits seemed like they went on forever, but all I could think about was Jay seeing my busted lip later on.

Truth be told, I didn't give a shit as long as I knew I would see him later on. At that moment, while my aunt fucked me up, I realized I was in love with Jay. I couldn't help myself. In my mind, the beating was worth every lick I took. The way he made me feel...it was so damn good—at the moment.

*****

They say love is a powerful drug, and I would tend to agree. Jay's love had me sick, head over heels, and stupid to my own thoughts. The bad thing about it is that I allowed him to know it. Just the thought of not having him sent me into a raging outburst. He was my drug, and I was addicted. I needed a full dose of him every night. He was my fix.

But like all drugs, there were side effects. I knew that, but nothing could have prepared me for the hotshot Jay became overnight. He gave me a dose of what being in love with him was all about!

*****

Heartbreak-

/Hârt Brãk/ - noun -overwhelming distress

OVERWHELMING DISTRESS
JAY

I knew things would get crazy after my aunt caught me sneaking Jay into the house, but damn—I didn't think it would get so hot in the kitchen.

She was knocking on doors and beefing with his momma. She was turning the heat up, acting like a complete savage out here in these Aliquippa streets. The more it escalated, the further he and I deteriorated.

Eventually, Jay began acting really strange. Over time, I saw him less and less, and before long he was ignoring all of my phone calls! We finally bumped into each other after countless nights he had left me alone. Just like a nigga to pull a disappearing act when the heat is turned up to one-hundred.

When I was with my girls I had to run down on that ass to be seen and heard. And of course, as soon as I saw that sexy grin all I fell for those dreamy eyes all over again. As was expected, he gave more excuses than the law allowed. I asked myself if I should even bother to listen to the lies, but I couldn't help myself. I had to indulge.

To my shock, the more I screamed, the calmer he became. In an attempt to diffuse the situation, he asked me into his cousin's house. I'd be lying if I said my pussy didn't get wet at the coolness surrounding his being. He wanted to chill. Unlike most people, I knew what that meant, so like the dummy I was, I went.

I was a little nervous, but my thot box was soaking wet as he took charge of the crisis at hand. The thought of being alone with him again was tantalizing to my inner spirit. As I was sitting there, I kept thinking to myself, *This is wrong, dead ass wrong. But he loves me, right? If loving him is so wrong, I don't ever want to be right.*

We started sipping that Henny and talking about a future together to kill the time. We both knew what we wanted, but we had to play around with the familiars to get through the awkwardness. Nothing else mattered in that moment. As if on cue,

Jay started kissing and touching all the right places. I was on fire, desperate for him, and he knew it.

Not wanting to wait any longer, I got undressed, seductively dancing in front of him. *The things we can do in this Cali king bed,* I thought to myself. *If these walls could talk, porn would pay to hear what they said.*

Slipping my fingers between my legs, I imagined your head devouring it.

"Are you hungry?" I whispered. Opening wider to make sure bae get fed, I made sure he said his grace gracefully as he bowed his head.

He had me soaking through the sheets, pulling on his dreads as he stole a piece of me all over again.

"Look me in my eyes," he ordered.

I knew at that moment that he had stole nothing—I had willingly given him everything.

Picking up the pace, my pussy left my juices running all down his face.

I was about to climax as my back arched with pleasure. Thrusting my head forward, my eyes rolled into the back of my head. Pinching my nipples, he did that little thing I like to my G-spot, making it hotter than ever.

Licking me clean, he thanked me for the ticking time bomb that had just exploded all down his face. Without another work, he flipped me over to assume the position.

Put it in the air, I allowed you to admire it. I could feel your pulsing manhood as you slid it up and down my birth canal. From the front to the back the succulent juices parade. Sliding your hands up my thighs, you forcefully spread my cheeks apart. I was drenched, ready for you to glide in as my favorite super hero and fuck me just the way you liked it. Like you owned it.

Like a match made in heaven my walls fit perfect around your throbbing vein as I clenched my attractions tight, while at the same time you were stroking me long and firm.

Within minutes, I had you moaning, calling me by name. Unable to contain yourself, you told me you loved this shit as you went a little deeper. Pushing harder, you dove farther into my love box I was throwing it back, ass shaking, knees buckling as I fell to the side. Giving me a firm smack, you attempted to keep me focused. I needed you to last a couple more minutes.

Baby, just a little longer. Slow down, I tell myself.

Rubbing my sensation faster and faster, I quickly exploded all over his manhood. As the spasms calm, I turn about and take him into my mouth, deep throating it sending the tip bouncing off my tonsils. I could tell by his moans that he about to blow it. Desperate for the taste of him, I added my special hand motion that I knew would be quick to cause his undoing. Sweet like honey, I let none go to waste.

Giving you a minute to catch your breath, I told you this love was gone have you gone. Hell yeah, mind blown.

At that moment I thought I had it all under control. What I would soon learn along my journey is that I rewarded a motherfucker for leaving me hanging, and then I gave him the permission to do it again when I expected the facts and lay down on my back.

I Waited

I waited for you to open your eyes and take a peek
I thought just maybe you'd see the slightest glimpse
of me.
Day after day
Night after night
I waited for you to notice me
Every time you opened your eyes, it wasn't me you
saw
That's just the harsh reality, yet I still waited.
I waited for you to realize that it was me in your
corner
Me that deserved you

But still you couldn't see.

I couldn't understand, for the death of me, what was

causing you to overlook me

I was standing there as tall as the towering tree

And still, YOU COULDN'T SEE ME

So yeah, I waited

I waited a little more

But how?

I mean, how can I keep this going when I knew it

wasn't me you saw

Even though I was standing as tall as the trees

Then it hit me

SHE!

She was the sun shining bright in the morning

The sun that rises and wakes you up

No wonder you couldn't see me

No matter how tall I tried to stand

There was just no competing.

I waited long enough

Only to hear you say there could be no you and me.

After all that was said and done I still couldn't see

You for who you were, I couldn't let you go
It was something in me that you needed
I made you feel free.
There was something I needed from you too
Love…

Naked

I'm standing here, naked as can be
When I say naked, I don't mean physically
I'm standing in front of you, my soul bleeding
Can't you see me
Or are you just too damn naïve
I gave you everything
Every single inch of me
I poured every ounce of love into you
For a moment, I thought your love was true
I fell heart-first and you let me hit the pavement
Like a ton of bricks, crashing foolishly
I thought you'd catch me

Hidden Secrets

I can't blame you
It was me—I was the one naïve
I didn't see the warning signs
It's safe to say I was blind
Looking through rose-colored blinds
Ain't no sense in crying
I find myself often falling for your kind
Emotionally unavailable hearts of unstable niggas
Barely able to love themselves
In turn, they couldn't possibly love anyone else
I'm always trying to fix a heart that I didn't break
Molding them into the man their momma shoulda
raised
Nah, ain't no tea nor shade
I'm just saying I always fall for this type of broken
man.

The Hottest Love and the Coldest End

The hottest love has the coldest end
I guess I'll be waiting for you, baby
In the wind
Still can't stomach that you and I had to end
You see, I loved you on days even when I couldn't
Love myself
When my mind told me I shouldn't
I put you up on the highest pedestal
Couldn't no nigga touch you

Hidden Secrets

Couldn't no nigga come through
What he did for me
Was something kind a magical
Especially spiritually, mentally, and emotionally
But while you sat high
I was low
Our love was far from on the same level and I knew
it
But you—
You did something to me that made my soul weak
You touched me and I'm not talking physically!
The hardest part was saying goodbye and letting go
But it was best for you and me
Tear-stained pillows
Painting pictures of your face
I'm up late at night thinking of you when I
shouldn't be
I know the thought of me being on your mind
couldn't be
Damn the hottest love had the coldest ending
How could this be.

I guess I'll be waiting for you in the wind.

Tired

She was tired and you could tell.

He was playing this game so well.

She had this look in her tearful eyes.

He wasn't man enough to swallow his pride.

She stayed and hoped things would change.

Sadly, he was content with things remaining this

way.

She often cried

More silent than not

He was so deep he couldn't stop.

She cared too much.

And he didn't care enough.

She was still head over heels in love.

He was different

No longer in love

She found it hard

But she had to leave

He didn't even look back when she finally walked

away!

Hidden Thoughts
THE THOUGHTS BEHIND MY SECRETS
TAKE FOUR

Just like that, I was back at square one; mind in turmoil and my heart broken beyond repair. Of course I let jay back in, and in doing so I uncovered a harsh world of truth. The longer I stayed, the more I realized the disrespect would continue.

I had to deal with women from the streets confronting me over and over again—many of them having been with his disrespectful ass as well. Those sweet lies that would roll off his tongue on cue, without a single thought, would play their part.

Each time I'd let him right back in. Just like that, I sent myself back into the flames he liked to call arms. That is, until that dreadful night everything took a turn for the worse during an argument about yet another chick. This time it was someone new.

His phone had been ringing nonstop, so I went through it. I tried to ignore it, making up excuses in my head. *Maybe it's just fiends calling, or maybe it's just the guys.* Like clockwork another call came through. Answering, some bitch named Tosha came across the line, screaming and yelling. From what I could gather between screams, he was late for a dick appointment.

"Can you believe this shit!" I screamed, throwing his phone across the room as he entered the door.

"Bitch, I'm getting real tired of constantly arguing with you every night," he mumbled through clenched teeth.

Ignoring the fact that his tone was colder than usual, I continued to talk my shit. "It's the same shit," I screamed over and over.

"You brought this on yourself," he shouted in return.

"I been nothing but loving—playing house, laid up in your mama's place. Haven't I?" I pressed, my anger rising. "You, on the other hand, you don't give a fuck about anyone but yourself. I'm going to work so I can make shit happen!" I sighed, my frustration rising. "All damn day and this is how you repay me! I'm sick of this shit, Jay. I'm lea—"

However, before I could finish my sentence, he hit me hard across the face. The taste of my own blood in my mouth brought me back to reality.

To this day, I can still feel his hand across my face, the sting upon my cheek.

Fighting back the tears that burned in my eyes, I stared at the man before me. The man I loved to the core of my being, my safe haven, the one I loved past any and everything, the one I cared for and cherished so deeply had lifted his hand to hit me! To harm ME! I never felt so low or crushed in my entire life.

I tried to fight back, but my punches landed on a hollow man. Nothing fazed him, not one hit! Angered, Jay continued punching me, one after the other, until I hit the ground. I thought he was finished with this brutal beating after I felt no more punches, but boy was I wrong. No sooner than I had that thought, he did the un-thinkable. Just then, his size 11 boots began kicking me all over. I tried to curl up into a ball, my precious baby in mind, but it was useless.

The look in his eyes was something I've never seen in any man walking this Earth! The flicker of love I thought he held for me was gone in an instant. Just like that, there was nothing left but cold black eyes, staring down at me.

To think, this is how he was treating me, knowing I was pregnant with his child, our child, the fruit of his loin! I really couldn't believe this was happening to me.

That night, as I lay bruised, face bloody, black and blue from the blows, soul breaking from the heartbreak of Jay, I made the decision that my unborn child would never know the man who had created it. It was better off that way. This was the end, the very last straw that I could take.

As I lay battered, I felt a sudden, sharp pain in my abdomen. It felt as though my whole body had been paralyzed, followed by a gush of blood rushing down my legs. Instantly, I began to panic! I knew it was still early on in the pregnancy, and after the continuous blows Jay had given me earlier in the day, I knew I was miscarrying.

Gathering all of the strength I could muster, I called for help, screaming for someone, anyone to help me! As I was waiting for help, I said a silent prayer. "Lord, I promise to do better. Please, just let my baby live. It deserves to live."

I guess my prayer had fallen on deaf ears. In that moment I lost all hope. There was no God above, no higher power!

All I remember is the ambulance rushing me to the ER as I fell in and out of consciousness. I could hear the doctors and nurses talking, saying that they couldn't find a heartbeat. When I finally awoke, I was surrounded by nurses, each sharing the same long face.

Eventually, a doctor finally spoke up telling me, "Sadly, there was nothing we could do. The trauma to the baby was too severe and it wouldn't make it."

Angered, I screamed at God. "How could you let this happen?" Truth is, I wasn't mad at God, I was mad at myself. How could *I* have let this happen? Why didn't I walk away sooner? If not for me, for the child I was carrying.

Hours later, after screaming and crying nonstop, I was defeated. As I was headed down the hall to get a DNC, the last remnants of a love so hot finally turned cold and would soon be scraped from my body. I could already feel in my soul that my baby was gone. The chance to have someone love me unconditionally had been taken away.

I knew after that day I'd never be the same. Nothing in my life would ever be the same as darkness filled my heart.

How was I supposed to pick up and just move on?

She Was Never

She wasn't a sweet dream
But a beautiful nightmare
She was never the pretty princess
She was Cruella DeVille
Yet, she was still beautiful.
No pink roses or sparking crowns
Just thistle bushes that rose from her ground
No fairy godmother with wands and magic
Just secret dungeons and fire breathing dragons
She loved being the wicked witch
So no one could hurt her
She vowed to remain closed off

Hidden Secrets

Long ago life turned her pure heart black and cold
Once upon a time, she used to shine bright with
love
Like gold reflecting in the sunshine
Then it dimmed that light with broken promises and
false hope
She's not who she thought
She let life mask her beauty
Wreaking havoc and chaos everywhere she's been
Who doesn't love a good girl turned villain?

Dear Momma

When it comes to my life
There was never a happy ending
Birth mother was a dope fiend
Godmother my world
I loved her till her death
But things weren't always what they seemed
I had a few sisters and brothers
But we were never close
Two aunts that were always down to ride for me
Friends who seemed to come and go
At ease for a minute
Had me feeling like it was me

Hidden Secrets

Always asked God why
Why can't there be somebody in my life that won't
flake
In 2008 I got a small bundle
That was great
Born an hour and forty-one minutes after eight
A gift no one could take
Always wanted to have a family
Thought I found it in that child's father
Come to find out that was fake
Moved on with my life
Was the best mother a young teen could be
Promised to always love and keep that baby
Since my mother never kept me
Finished school
Went off to try and get my degree
Had a minor set back
A heartbreak that made my soul ache
The mere thought still makes my heart crack
But that's not it
Hold on—just wait

Chick had me ready to hurt me, myself, looking
back I was in a toxic state.
But here comes my Superman to put shit back in-
place,
To mend my broken heart
But all that shit was fake.
Found out shortly after that there was another
heartbeat growing inside me
How clever
I welcomed my second love on June 19, 2013
Shortly after three
Again, y'all heard me say I wanted a family
I guess keeping him and having a family meant
losing my sanity
Wondering what you're doing
Who you're with
Will I see you at home tonight?
That just didn't sit right
He was always in them streets
Never living right
Found something in bitches that scratched that itch

Hidden Secrets

The crave of a love for my own
Learned the hard way about chicks
You can give their ass the world
It won't mean shit
The rest of this is unwritten.

Ten More Doors

You huffed and puffed and blew down that first
wall
Only to find there were ten more doors
Before you would be able to peek at my soul
Yet, you stay outside that wall
Strategizing on how you would demolish them all to
get to me
As you got to wall five
I got kind of shaky
Could you possibly go through all of this if you
didn't plan to love me?
When you got to door six

Hidden Secrets

I started shifting

Somewhere along that shift I lost traction and I

began to fall

This man is getting closer

Nervousness is setting in

Am I ready to truly let you in?

You see, this is nothing that I am used to

Most didn't get this far

I pushed them away

I've used this technique for years

'Cause I hate to feel pain

Shutting them out is my only way of staying safe

Oh no, you have reached door eight

You are only two doors away of seeing my heart

Seeing the scars that it holds from things in my life

I begin to pray to God

"Oh, Lord, he's breaching door nine

My father, please help me

What do I do next?

"Breathe, my child, you have got to have faith "

"Oh, Lord, I'm just not that great

Unique Writez

"My child, I created you and I make no mistakes"
I do not deserve this man
Oh, God, he's standing at door ten
And as that wall tumbles down piece by piece
He began to hold my heart so delicately
As if it were a piece of artwork
He stared at it as though it were priceless
Speaking words of hopes and promises
This time I have fallen and it's like a breath of fresh
air
I'm sitting on a cloud with fears of falling down
I've let him in
What am I gonna do now?

I Think

As hard as it may be
I think it's about time I faced the harsh reality
I'm in love with you.
Truth is, you're not in love with me.
Yes, you heard that correctly.
You're not in love with me.
I can feel the chilling distance between us
Even though you're right next to me.
I saw all the warning signs before it got this far.
Instead of letting go, I just blamed me.
It had to be me, right?
Lying here right now

Unique Writez

In the dead of the night
The vibe isn't right
Maybe you're not ready
It may not be our time
Is that hard to admit you're afraid to throw in the
towel?
Call it quits?
If you're not in love
How do you benefit from this relationship?

Something Special

He was something different
Something special
More like the sunset across the beach
His kiss the sweet breeze

I get nervous around him
His touch sends a chill I wonder if he's ever
noticed.
Every time I'm with him
I can't focus
Lost in the moment

I love that he expresses his emotions
I never have to second-guess if I'm wanted
His actions correspond with every word he's told
me
So patient and understanding
He understands me.
He's the kind of man that makes your blood rush
and face blush

The feeling he gives me is crazy
I can't explain it
Daydreaming about him on the daily
Had me feeling crazy

This Guy

This guy makes stutter, stumble, and mumble when
in his presence.
The essence of this guy makes every single nerve
tingle.
I'm crushing!
Wish I could muster up the courage to let this guy
know.
The calmness of his being makes my heart stop
beating.
I'm nervous
I just let him walk by without speaking
Just do it, I whisper to myself.

This guy is the epitome of a handsome black man.

He's artfully sculpted with mocha stained skin.

I'm infatuated with him

I wonder if he can tell I sit and gawk over him.

How when the breeze caresses my cheek, I wish it

were his lips.

As I lie in bed, thoughts of him drift around in my

head

I dream of him

This guy is such a King

A male reflection of me

I just wanna speak into him, life and positivity.

If only I could speak without choking

"Hello," the words spilled out like vomit with out

me thinking

He looked up and smiled

It was so captivating, it made me shy

"I've been dying to meet you. Why don't you sit for

a while," he said.

Enough

I'm sorry I wasn't enough
I hope the next woman you're with, you're able to
treat her good
I'm sorry we didn't make it
Communication lacked abuse and became all too
much
I used to blame myself thinking you were just as
misunderstood
I pray for the all the women who cross your
treacherous path
Maybe you won't take them for granted
I'm sorry it had to end so abruptly

Some things just aren't meant to be

The road was just too tough

I'm not sorry we had to let go and give it up

I only have one thing left to say

May God have mercy someday he may change who

you are

I hope you don't mind, I kept a piece of your heart

as a token

But as you know I couldn't stay

You didn't deserve me

Not then

Not now.

Enough was enough!

I had to leave my broken heart behind

I had to forgive me for not loving myself more.

I had to go through everything I had to go through

In order for me to stand here.

For me to have the courage to let you see through

me

My heart in human form

Emotional and emotionless from the hidden
thoughts deep within
The thoughts behind my secrets.

Almost

How was I supposed to pick up and move on? I had so much loss to mourn—I'd lost a lover and a friend. I'd lost the unborn child he gave me, by his hand. I was empty. I had nothing left to give as I stood in quicksand. I was sinking. The days were quickly moving into different seasons but I wasn't living. I was nothing more than a hollow shell, a black hole swallowing me. I felt like I could no longer breath. Everything hurt from the inside-out.

I guess it's true what they say—heartbreak can be physical. I felt it deep in my bones, all the way into my soul. The negative emotions set in like a cancer, swiftly growing and nearly unstoppable. I'd never felt this kind of hurt in my life. I couldn't eat anything, although I made my attempts. Sadly, it came right back up. I tried to talk about it, but it seemed like no one on earth understood.

Nobody can understand that empty feeling swarming around in their gut until they have experienced what it feels like when the heart doesn't break even. It's a selfish emotion, which consumes your body, mind, and spirit. In a way, being in love is an addiction; it triggers the same nerves in your brain as an addictive substance. That's why you crave your significant other's soul when they leave you.

In my time of despair, I desperately needed someone—someone to save me from this pit, to save me from myself. I was alone and there was no help. Eventually, I began to have thoughts of suicide! It was the only solution I could come up with to ease my suffering. The way I saw it, it would end the world of pain that was completely crippling me.

I knew I had a son to look after, but I figured he would eventually understand that he was better off without out me. Even though he was the light of my life, the last bit I had left in this world, somehow the darkness would always find a way to pull me in, completely consuming me. I couldn't take how much darkness existed within me.

This is it—this is the end of me. I'm going to end it all very soon. Those closest to me will understand that I tried as best as I could to move on, to move forward.

Unfortunately, the pain was so crippling, ripping through me. It was like an illness spreading rapidly, infecting all of those near me. *God, if this is what death is, take me now. Free me from this hell that I'm living*, I silently prayed, as if he were listening.

I'd need him to stop what I was going to do by intervening in some type of way. If he didn't, I'd be merely a memory. Instead, they'd tell tales of who I used to be or who they thought I used to be.

Growing up, from the time I was 12 or 13, I was never the happy girl; never carefree. It was never a breeze or a walk in the park like many children my age. Even into adulthood with a child of my own, every man I slept with thrust me back to my childhood. I could still smell the stale stench of cigarettes my uncle had on his breath as he molested me. The feeling of his clammy drunken hands across my young body left me with a feeling of disgust. After that, sex would never the same. Hell, life would never be the same. My innocence had been snatched, and of course no one believed me. Not even the man who gave me life—the man who was supposed to always protect me.

It was because of the horrors of my childhood, that I found myself in the arms of what I thought was love. Instead, he was an abuser, a master manipulator, a calculated narcissist. Not only had he damn near killed me physically, he had succeeded in killing me mentally and emotionally.

The Henny tingles the back of my throat as I take shot after shot, dancing with the devil. My body consumes the fire, thriving on it. Reaching for the bottle of pills on the dresser, I pray for them to assist my alcohol hero. Life wasn't worth living if this is what I had to deal with. I'd rather be gone than unhappy, boxing with the intoxicating seeds planted within me.

Mind made up, I sent out texts that this would be my last night. *No more pain*, I thought as I took the hand full of pills, leaned back, and relaxed.

My Faith is Still Tested!

All of this is what it took to get here, to get back to me—the real me.

I used to question if God existed. If he did, why did I have to go through all of this? I have days where my faith is still tested, but I've learned faith and prayer without work means nothing.

I made it through the fire, so I'm proof of that. I am who I am today because of how bad he tested my faith. Mother, student, mentor, entrepreneur—I wear many hats. However, after hearing my story many can't believe that I lost it all. I was broken down to my core, stripped of everything except my life.

Through the help of the Lord, I was finally able to open my eyes. I'm no longer just the broken little brown girl, I'm the strongest woman alive, ready to tackle the world. If I had to do it all again, I wouldn't dare take away the pain. That's what made me who I am. After all, you can't have sunshine without a little rain every now and again. Now, that doesn't meant it doesn't get rough. Just remember, that's just God testing me, testing us. If I fail, I get back up and try again because deep down, I know with him by my side, there is absolutely no battle I can't win.

Sincerely Yours,
The Unbroken Girl

What's Next at Emotional Fiction Publishing

MRS. & MRS. TOXIC
BY: NIKKI FLOWERS
Available Now

I fell to my knees in dying need of a pill to help me bleed and cope with every emotion I came into contact with. I've tried to drink them away. I tried to sleep them away. I've tried to mast them in hopes they would go away! Now, I just say f*ck it and force myself to live with them. Am I the reject version of a superhero?!

Emotionally, I rise to help other, I crawl to my familiars, and I wear a cape to protect my emotional state of mind. I am a pillar.

Intoxicating moments throughout good and bad memories created both good and bad intentions within every relationship I created.

Once my emotional state was born, I fell in love with Mrs. Toxic. The Mrs. Toxic I stared at in the mirror was the same Mrs. Toxic who stared back.

*****

THE SHADOWS OF A MAN
BY: JAMES MINARD-SELLERS

"The Shadows are the hellacious levels of my life. It changes as life rearranges. There is always a story in the Shadows, as well as my reflection"

I was raised to love respect and protect my siblings at any cost. That's what my father told me every time he punched me in the chest, knocking the wind out of me and leaving me on the floor, gasping for air. I was 3 years old. He started beating, or as he called it, instilling, into me what I was there for—to take care of my mother and my sisters. He taught me how to fight, shoot, and use knives. I was the oldest boy, but the fourth youngest child. There were 3 girls born before me.

"It is your job to protect them, love them, and to do so until death," my father would tell me over and over and over. My father was an Army Sergeant and a member of The Black Panther Movement. Despite the fact that mother would often tell him to, 'Stop hitting on him like he is a grown-ass man. It will make him hard,' he refused to do so. With each new beating he would tell me to get up and that I better not cry. Once I was on my feet he would punch me directly in the stomach to test my resolve. Still, despite my mother's arguments, she agreed—I was there to take care of her and my sisters.

Once daddy was gone, the words were spoken and slapped into by my mother. However, it was around that time the sexual molestation from my first cousins became worse. I was 4 years old when it all began, and I allowed them to do so in order to protect my baby brothers and sisters. I gave up my mental and physical freedom for them. After all, it was my job to protect them. I lied, stole, and even killed in their name. I sold my body to provide our Christmases, Easters, and our Thanksgivings.

My father had put me in the mental position and mother had put me in a physical one, which held the responsibility of a grown man, not a 14-year-old boy. And when I needed them at my darkest hour, they weren't there. Not a single one of them! It destroyed me. I had made sacrifices my entire life, and endured more pain for my family and from my family than anyone should ever have to take. The pure love I had inside quickly turned to hate.

Though, deep down, I loved them at any cost. Even if that meant selling my body at the age of fourteen to feed my younger brothers and sister, and to supply my mother's free-base habit, as well as my own.

This is just the beginning of the Shadows that groomed me into the man I am today. Come and walk with me through the shadows of death, which helped to bring me back to life.

*****

JIVE TURKEY, BULL CRAP, AND MONKEY BUSINESS AS USUAL
BY: EVANS F. HARVEY

It had to be a lifetime on drugs and doing crimes.
Drug binges out of control
Using drugs and dropping dimes.
Everything is for sale
Stolen merchandise, fifty percent off.
Everything's going half price.

Prison was hard
Got caught a few times.

In it for the high
I did 8 years for petty crimes.
Many nights missing the pipe and flame
Getting higher than the clouds hoping I didn't get
caught in the rain.

Burned so many bridges
Glass and fire
Addict to crack
Ball and chain
Crack women are magicians
Dope fiend's magic
Crack gone
Dope missing from your gadget

Hard to imagine me on dope
Flames so high the glass pipe broke
Dope to the pipe
Flame up that fire
Smoked out all night
Burned out 10 BIC lighters

Morals on respirator

Scheme and scam

This dope got me hooked, and it don't give a

damn.

I dug a hole for myself

I'm one foot from six

I'd be damn if I have to die in this bitch

It's my dirt, so I gotta cover up this ditch.

Under the radar

I stayed on the police shit list.

Mind over matter

But the matter got my mind.

In it for the high so nothing valuable was ever

mine

To be truthful with you, I didn't feel like dying

You say a try beats a blank

I nearly gave up trying

It felt like the world stopped spinning when I
started doping
My world began spinning again when I started
coping.
Sometimes you gotta burn a bridge to build
bridges.

I survived pains that melt tall men to midgets!
I still got good memories in the cold where it's
frigid.
Those same memories make it easy for me to miss
it.
Through the pain and suffering—I never miss
that.

From the gutter to gravy
My greatest comeback!

*****

MULATTA NOBODY
BY: ALETHEA JIMISON

I was always a quiet child
Very withdrawn and shy
I lived in my endless imagination
Flying winged horses in the sky.
Creaking attic boards were the background beat
To pattering little mulatta feet.
I learned to be invisible as a child
So as not to draw attention
From sour faces of judgment and bitter
dispositions.
When I was a child, I didn't know why grandma
glared at us
When we tried to be quiet
While playing with our toys.
I never understood why my mother held her
tongue
Like a whipped angel with brittle poise.
I felt like a mulatta nobody watching my shining
cousins laughing freely

While my siblings and I sat away from the family
like quiet quaking leaves.
You see, my cousins shined like fairy-tale princes
and princesses to me.
Golden, shimmering hair
A dimple here and there
And most certainly white luminous skin.
Like every doll I owned,
They mocked me unknowingly.
I had a doll with red hair, blond hair and….
Wait—there is one with brown hair…like me.
Actually, she has blue eyes like my cousin.
There were no mulatta dolls with skin like honey
And eyes like almonds
Because grandpa said we were made of sin.
In the creaking attic we crept
Like little shadows,
Hoping to go unnoticed by silent condemnation
Which seemed louder than the attempt to smother
the sounds
Of little mullata feet.

About Unique Writez

Facebook Group: https://bit.ly/2JK8XMy
Instagram: _theperfectflaw
Twitter: ThePerfect_Flaw
Facebook: https://bit.ly/2JElroV

You can contact Unique Writez at
asiahhayes@gmail.com

Unique Writez, born Asiah Hayes, was born and raised on the outskirts of Pittsburgh in the small city of Aliquippa.

Being from such a small town and having already been through the ringer in life, Unique began to use writing as her coping mechanism. Falling in love with the way her words flowed through the pen, each stroke began telling a story! Unique had big dreams that one day her writings would touch many.

A single mother of three, with nothing to lose, Unique began her journey with Emotional

Fiction Publishing Firm. Sending everything she had, in hopes it was good enough to be signed, she completed her first book in 2019 titled, *Hidden Thoughts: The Thoughts Behind My Secrets.*

Made in the USA
Middletown, DE
09 June 2019